ROBERT BURNS

Text by
Kenneth Simpson

Colin Baxter Photography Ltd, Grantown-on-Spey, Scotland

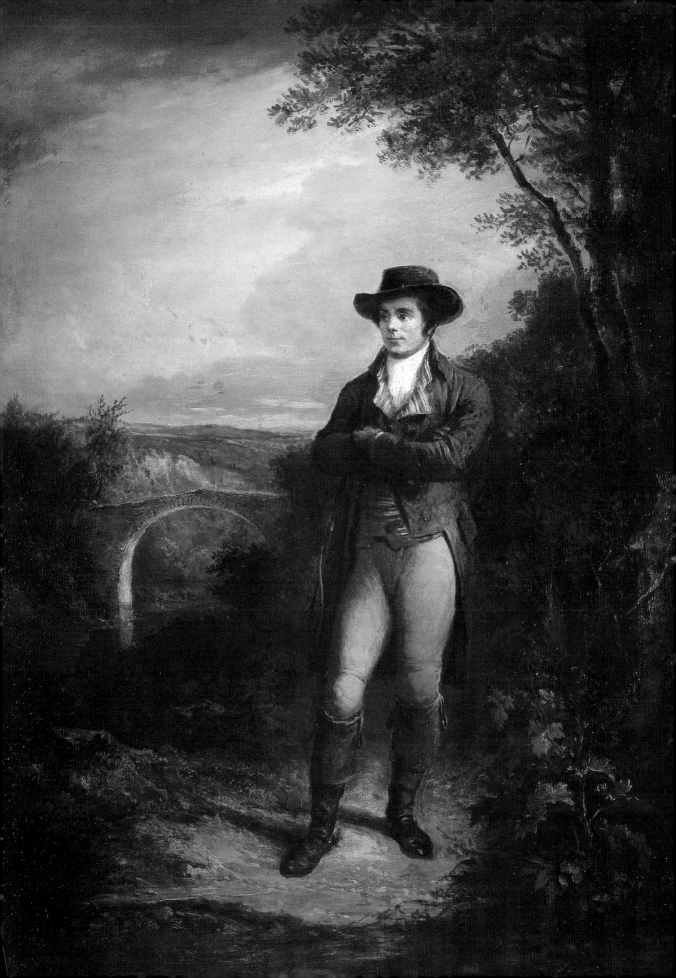

Early Life, Education and Early Manhood

Our monarch's hindmost year but ane
Was five and twenty days begun,
'Twas then a blast o' Janwar Win'
Blew hansel in on Robin.

A few days after the birth of Robert Burns on 25 January 1759 a storm damaged the roof of the Alloway cottage, his birthplace. William Burnes took his wife and infant son to a neighbour's, returning to repair the damage.

The storm was perhaps a portent. Burns's personal life was turbulent: 'There's ae wee faut they whiles lay to me;/ I like the lasses – Gude forgie me!' he wrote in 'Epistle to John Lapraik, An Old Scotch Bard', and he would prove it by fathering thirteen children. Burns would also take the literary world by storm. His output was remarkable: from a life of 37 years came over 600 poems and songs, and over 700 letters are extant.

What is the reason for Burns's appeal? Partly it lies in the breadth of his work. His chameleon gifts as poet ensure that there is something to which everyone can relate. It is the same Burns who writes satires on social injustice and laments in verse the severing of the stem of a daisy or the overturning of a mouse's nest. But it is the values that he espouses that make him world-renowned. 'My two favourite topics [are] Love and Liberty', he wrote in a letter in 1793. These informed his life and his writing. Acknowledging his 'old powerful foes, the Devil, the World, and the Flesh', in a letter in February 1788, he lived life to the full. His championing of liberty would lead to suspicion as to his politics, threatening his career in the Excise. He wrote to Mrs. Frances Dunlop on 3 April 1789, 'Politics is dangerous ground for me to tread on, and yet I cannot for the soul of me resist an impulse of any thing like Wit'. The freedom he sought led him to identify the liberating power of the imagination with that of the arch-rebel, Satan himself. In a letter of February 1787 to James Dalrymple, Burns commented, 'I suppose the devil is so elated at his success...in making you a poet'. It is no coincidence that it was Burns who wrote 'The Deil's awa wi' the Exciseman'; and it is revealing that the description of the storm in 'Tam o' Shanter' ends as follows: 'That night, a child might understand,/ The Deil had business on his hand'.

William Burnes (1721-1784), a native of Kincardineshire, moved south for work. After two years in Edinburgh he came to Ayrshire and soon became head gardener on the Doonholm estate of Dr. William Fergusson. He rented 7 acres from Alexander Campbell on which he built 'the auld clay biggin' (so Burns terms it in 'The Vision'). At Maybole fair in 1756 he met Agnes Broun (1732-1820) of Kirkoswald, and they married on 15 December 1757. Robert was the eldest of seven children, the others being Gilbert (1760), Agnes (1762), Annabella (1764), William (1767), John (1769), and Isabella (1771).

Parental influences were strong. From his mother Burns had his first contact with Scots song; and lodging with them was her cousin, Betty Davidson, of whom Burns wrote in his autobiographical letter of 2 August 1787: 'She had...the largest collection in the county of tales and songs concerning devils, ghosts, fairies, brownies, witches, warlocks, spunkies, kelpies, elf-candles, dead-lights, wraiths, apparitions, cantraips, giants, inchanted towers, dragons, and other trumpery. This cultivated the latent seeds of Poesy'. The legacy is evident from such poems as 'Halloween', 'Address to the Deil', and 'Tam o' Shanter'.

William Burnes was a firm believer in education. He compiled a 'Manual of Religious Belief' for his family and he

up favorite quotations, and store them in my mind as ready armour, offensive or defensive, amid the struggle of this turbulent existence', he told Mrs. Dunlop, 6 December 1792. There is no writer who is more obviously the sum of his reading; there is no writer who made more effective use of his reading.

In 1766 the family moved to Mount Oliphant farm on the Doonholm estate. William Burnes tutored his children when the day's work was over, and in the summer of 1772 Robert and Gilbert went in alternate weeks to Dalrymple School. When John Murdoch returned to Ayr Grammar School in 1773 Burns lodged with him for three weeks, attending classes in English and French and attempting some Latin. If the hours of schooling seem slight, they are more than offset by the parent's dedication to education and the avid learning of the child. Burns continued to devour books throughout his adult life; visitors remarked that he had a book by him even at meals.

ensured that his sons had as much education as the demands of the farm allowed. Burns's song, 'My Father was a Farmer' pays tribute to him: 'My father was a farmer upon the Carrick border, O/ And carefully he bred me in decency and order, O'; and the depiction of family life in 'The Cotter's Saturday Night' owes something to his father's influence. In 1765 Robert and Gilbert attended William Campbell's school at Alloway. Then William Burnes and four others hired as a tutor the eighteen-year-old John Murdoch, son of the Auchinleck schoolmaster. The early emphasis was on reading, writing, memorising poems and hymns, and elements of rhetoric. Murdoch's recollection of his pupils' talents is surprising: 'Gilbert always appeared to me to possess a more lively imagination, and to be more of the wit, than Robert'. Equally puzzling is his comment that Robert's 'ear [was] remarkably dull, and his voice untuneable'. However William Burnes predicted, 'Whoever may live to see it, something extraordinary will come from that boy'. He was right: Burns possessed extraodinary gifts, in particular the 'retentive memory' he mentioned in his letter to Dr John Moore. Once read or heard, a poem or song was with him always. 'I pick

day's work was over, and in the summer of 1772 Robert and Gilbert went in alternate weeks to Dalrymple School. When John Murdoch returned to Ayr Grammar School in 1773 Burns lodged with him for three weeks, attending classes in English and French and attempting some Latin. If the hours of schooling seem slight, they are more than offset by the parent's dedication to education and the avid learning of the child. Burns continued to devour books throughout his adult life; visitors remarked that he had a book by him even at meals.

Life at Mount Oliphant was hard. The soil was unfertile and Burns later described the farm as 'a ruinous bargain'. Gilbert recalled conditions: 'To the buffetings of misfortune, we could only oppose hard labour and the most rigid economy. We lived very sparingly. For several years butcher's meat was a stranger in the house...[Robert] at fifteen was the principal labourer on the farm, for we had no hired servants...I doubt not but the hard labour and sorrow of this period...was in a great measure the cause of that depression of spirits with which Robert was so often afflicted through his whole life'. After the death of William Fergusson – 'my father's generous master' as Burns described him – the estate was controlled by a less benign factor who harried the tenants. He inspired these lines of Caesar in 'The Twa Dogs':

> Poor tenant-bodies, scant o' cash,
> How they maun thole a factor's snash;
> He'll stamp an' threaten, curse an' swear,
> He'll apprehend them, poind their gear;
> While they maun stan', wi' aspect humble,
> An' hear it a', an' fear an' tremble.

Early in life Burns experienced the inhumanity to one's fellow-beings that would prompt his satires.

Life for the adolescent was not all gloom however. His partner at harvesting in 1774, Nellie Kilpatrick, provided his first romantic encounter and inspired his first composition, the song 'O once I loved a Bonny Lass'. 'I...committed the sin of RHYME' he wrote, adding, 'she...initiated me in a certain delicious Passion...Thus with me began Love and Poesy'. In his note on the song in his *First Commonplace Book* Burns wrote, 'I never had the least thought or inclination of turning Poet till I got once heartily in Love, and then Rhyme and Song were, in a manner, the spontaneous language of my heart'.

The summer of 1775 saw Burns return to more formal schooling. Eleven weeks were spent at Hugh Rodger's school in Kirkoswald studying surveying. With fellow-pupils Hugh Niven and Thomas Orr, he would debate the ways of the world. Rodger once challenged Burns to a debate on the issue of whether a general or a merchant was the more valuable member of society. Burns was willing to take either side; Rodger opted for

the general, leaving his pupil to argue the case for the merchant, which he did so effectively as to be acclaimed the victor. Plainly John Murdoch's teaching of rhetoric had made its mark. Burns's later letters to his former school-mates – termed by him his 'Literary Correspondence' - reflect the young man's rather studied seriousness and offer views not always in keeping with the popular image of Burns: on 17 November 1782 Burns wrote, 'I love to see a man who has a mind superior to the world and the world's men – a man who, conscious of his own integrity, and at peace with himself, despises the censures and opinions of the unthinking rabble of mankind'.

The school at Kirkoswald brought further romance. In August, 'a month which is always a carnival in my bosom' he told Moore, 'a charming Fillette who lived next door to the school overset my Trigonometry, and set me off in a tangent from the sphere of my studies'. She was Margaret (Peggy) Thomson, referred to as 'My fair, my lovely charmer' in 'Song Composed in August'.

At Whitsun 1777 William Burnes acquired the lease of Lochlie Farm at 20 shillings an acre from David McClure, an Ayr merchant. 'For four years we lived comfortably', Burns later wrote. His social

Robert Burns's Cottage at Alloway by Sam Bough:
William Burnes held the feu-titles of the cottage until 1781 when they were purchased for £160 by the Corporation of Shoemakers of Ayr. The premises were used as an inn for many years, but in 1847 an extension was built for Burns manuscripts and artefacts. In 1881 the Trustees bought the cottage and grounds for £4000.

Outdoor Dance in Nithsdale – engraving from Land o' Burns: Burns is a great celebrant of communal rural life, indoor or outdoor. In 'Epistle to John Lapraik, an Old Scotch Bard' he records a winter night's party: 'On Fasteneen we had a rockin,/ To ca' the crack and weave our stockin;/ And there was muckle fun and jokin,/ Ye need na doubt;/ At length we had a hearty yokin,/ At sang about'. From spring to autumn communal dances outdoors were a highlight of rural life. Burns's responsiveness to the rhythms of dance is evident from various of his poems and songs. These lines in 'Tam o' Shanter' enact their meaning: 'The piper loud and louder blew;/ The dancers quick and quicker flew;/ They reel'd, they set, they cross'd, they cleekit'.

circle expanded and, as 'the most ungainly, awkward being in the parish', he set about polishing his social skills. Attendance at a Tarbolton dancing-class was 'in absolute defiance of [his father's] commands'. Paternal disapproval probably exacerbated his son's behaviour: Burns wrote, 'from that instance of rebellion he took a kind of dislike to me, which I believe was one cause of that dissipation which marked my future years'. On his death-bed, 13 February 1784, William Burnes revealed that there was only one member of his family about whose future conduct he was concerned – Robert.

On 11 November 1780 Burns and six other young men founded the Tarbolton Bachelors' Club for 'diversion, to relieve the wearied man worn down with the necessary labours of life'. Of the rules, the tenth is the most significant: 'Every man proper for a member of this Society, must have a frank, honest, open heart; above anything dirty or mean; and must be a professed lover of one or more of the female sex. No haughty, self-conceited person, who looks upon himself as superior to the rest of the Club, and

especially no mean-spirited, worldly mortal, whose only will is to heap up money shall upon any pretence whatever be admitted' - this reads like Burns's personal manifesto. Joining the Club a year later was David Sillar, to whom Burns later addressed 'Epistle to Davie'. On 4 July 1781 Burns became a Freemason with his induction into Tarbolton Lodge, where he would become Depute Master on 27 July 1784.

During 1780-81 Burns courted Elizabeth Gebbie (thought by some to be called Alison Begbie), who inspired the song 'The Lass of Cessnock Banks'. When she rejected him he praised her warm, feeling heart, though his later account of the experience suggests real hurt: 'a belle-fille whom I adored and who had pledged her soul to meet me in the field of matrimony, jilted me with peculiar circumstances of mortification'. Recollection of the episode prompted the song, 'Fair Eliza'.

In July 1781 Burns went to Irvine, then the largest town in Ayrshire, to learn flax-dressing from Alexander Peacock, a relative of his mother with premises in Glasgow Vennel. It proved 'a sadly ruinous affair' as his partner was 'a scoundrel of the first water', and during New Year celebrations a fire burnt the heckling-shop to the ground. Like many a young person, Burns felt the stresses of embarking on a new career, remote from home and in a larger community than he had known, and in the last three months of 1781 his health deteriorated. Suffering from what would now be termed clinical depression, he was visited five times in eight days (14-22 November) by Dr. Charles Fleeming. To his father, understandably concerned, Burns wrote on 27 December, 'The weakness of my nerves has so debilitated my mind that I dare not, either review past events, or look forward into futurity...I am quite transported at the thought that ere long, perhaps very soon, I shall bid an eternal adieu to all the pains & uneasiness & disquietudes of this weary life'. The legacy of such black depression surfaces in 'Remorse' and 'Despondency: An Ode'.

1782 saw a lifting of his spirits. He resumed flax-dressing, but with a new partner; and he befriended Richard Brown, a native of Irvine six years his senior, later the captain of a West Indiaman. On walks in Eglinton Woods Burns recited his poems to Brown who recommended he submit them for publication. He was also a mentor in matters of the heart, being, Burns told Moore, 'the only man I ever saw who was a greater fool than myself when WOMAN was the presiding star'.

Leaving Irvine 'like a true poet, not worth a sixpence', Burns returned to Lochlie in the spring of 1782 and his health improved. He read voraciously. After Kirkoswald he had read the poems of James Thomson and William Shenstone; and the novels *Tristram Shandy*, by Laurence Sterne, and Henry Mackenzie's *The Man of Feeling* became his 'bosom favorites', giving him models of, respectively, whimsical and earnest sensibility. He returned from Irvine with two volumes of Richardson's *Pamela* and one of *Ferdinand Count Fathom* by fellow-Scot, Tobias Smollett, to whose 'incomparable humor' he alluded in a letter of 18 July 1788. But it was the poems of Robert Fergusson (1750-1774) that particularly inspired Burns: 'meeting with Fergusson's Scotch Poems, I strung anew my wildly-sounding rustic lyre with emulating vigour'. Greatly admiring Fergusson's poetry, and lamenting his death, Burns commissioned the erection of a stone in February 1787 – for which he composed the epigraph – to mark Fergusson's grave in Canongate cemetery. Burns paid the architect, Robert Burn, five years later, explaining in a letter of 5 February 1792, 'He was two years in erecting it, after I commissioned him for it; and I have been two years paying him, after he sent me his account; so he and I are quits'.

In April 1783 Burns started his *First Commonplace Book*. It seems likely that he already had an eye on publication as he projects an image of himself: 'As he was but little indebted to scholastic education, and bred at a plough-tail, his performances must be strongly tinctured with his unpolished, rustic way of life'. The paradox of masquerading as an untutored rustic in formal Augustan prose is a telling one; and the key word is 'performances' since many of Burns's poems were precisely that, the work of a sophisticated literary artist. His letters, too, he described as 'epistolary performances' in a letter of 26 March 1787.

Tarbolton. Procession of St. James Lodge, 1846 (from a painting by D.O. Hill): Freemasonry thrived in late-eighteenth-century Scotland, possibly because it resonated with Scottish Enlightenment ideals of personal and social improvement; and, recruiting from a broad range of occupations, it chimed with Scottish egalitarian notions. Burns's fellow-masons in Ayrshire included Sir John Whiteford, master of St. James's Lodge, Gavin Hamilton, John Ballantine, Provost of Ayr, Professor Dugald Stewart, Dr. John Mackenzie of Mauchline, and William Dalrymple of Orangefield. They were instrumental in subscribing for, and publicising, the Kilmarnock edition. John Wilson, schoolmaster in Tarbolton, ran a grocer's shop where he also sold medicines. It was his talk on medical matters to the local Lodge which prompted Burns's satiric portrait of the amateur apothecary in 'Death and Dr. Hornbook'. In Edinburgh Burns was made a member of Canongate Kilwinning Lodge No. 2. Among the members who would influence Burns's career and social life were his patron, the Earl of Glencairn, the Earl of Eglinton, Patrick Miller of Dalswinton, lawyer Alexander Cunningham, schoolmaster William Nicol, Creech the publisher, Henry Mackenzie, and Alexander Nasmyth.

'Very Busy with the Muses': The Mossgiel Years

On 17 May 1783 a writ of sequestration was served on William Burns by David McClure. Concerned for the family's future, Robert and Gilbert privately sub-leased the 118-acre Mossgiel Farm outside Mauchline at £90 per year from Gavin Hamilton, a patron and friend of Burns. On 27 January 1784 the father won his appeal at the Court of Session but, weakened by tuberculosis, he died a few weeks later. After his burial in Alloway's old kirkyard – where Burns later inscribed an epitaph – the family returned briefly to Lochlie before moving to Mossgiel in March.

Despite his commitment to the farm Burns was now prolific as a poet. In February 1786 he could justifiably claim, 'I have been very busy with the muses'. Rural life provided him with material, but he does not simply hold a mirror to reality; rather he uses specific experience as the basis of subtle commentaries on human

nature. The earliest example was a poem composed in 1782 while still at Lochlie. A tethered ewe fell over on its back and, to Burns's amusement, his farm-worker was helpless as to what to do. The incident prompted Burns to write that very day 'The Death and Dying Words of Poor Mailie, the Author's Only Pet Yowe, an Unco' Mournfu' Tale'. It is a brilliant blend of animal fable and 'last dying words' tradition (Burns may have been influenced by Allan Ramsay's 'Lucky Spence's Last Advice' the valediction of an Edinburgh brothel-keeper). In a comic role-reversal the dumb-struck peasant, Huoc, is addressed by the highly articulate sheep. In her last message to her master Mailie reveals herself as a mistress of contradiction. Apparently she has read Rousseau on the merits of natural education, and she has a sound economic sense derived perhaps from Adam Smith.

Mossgiel Farm: attributed to William Bartlett

Portrait (1787) by Alexander Nasmyth Nasmyth's first portrai Burns, for which the pe attended sittings at the artist's lodgings in War Court, was engraved by Beugo (1759-1841) fo (1787) Edinburgh editi poems. Burns wrote or February 1787, 'I am g my Phiz done by an en Engraver; and if it can ready in time, I will ap in my book looking, lik other fools, to the title page'. Gilbert Burns lat wrote that he thought engraving captured the better than the origina painting; and Nasmyth, took no fee, expressed preference for a later engraving by Walker.

and daughter is to stay in the parish, mixing with well-reared youngsters like herself:

> O, may thou ne'er forgather up,
> Wi' onie blastet, moorlan toop;
> But ay keep mind to moop an' mell,
> Wi' sheep o' credit like thysel!

From the mouth of a sheep, well-read and well-bred, Burns highlights the human tendency to espouse principles in the abstract but then do otherwise when personally involved. At first glance the poem seems a comic account, but it sustains an acute insight into human behaviour.

Equally rooted in personal, though poignant, circumstances is 'The Twa Dogs. A Tale'. Begun in 1784 as tribute to Burns's dog Luath, killed on the eve of his father's death, it was completed by February 1786. A poem whose antecedents might seem to be in Robert Henryson's *Fables* develops into a social satire of the times. Though their masters are, respectively, aristocrat and peasant-farmer, Caesar (a retriever) and Luath (a ploughman's collie) share a language, vernacular Scots, and a fellowship denied class-ridden human society. Their discussion of the life-styles of their owners demonstrates Burns's mastery of dialogue and rhetoric. To Caesar's pitying descriptions of the wretched lot of the peasantry Luath responds not with the agreement Caesar expects but an acknowledgement of the compensations that hard work brings. Eventually, however, he concedes one of Caesar's claims:

> There's monie a creditable stock
> O' decent, honest, fawsont folk,
> Are riven out baith root an' branch,
> Some rascal's pridefu' greed to quench.

Thereafter, Luath begins to control the direction of their debate. Caesar responds, 'Haith lad, ye little ken about it', and elaborates on the debauchery of the upper classes. By ending his next contribution

The Jolly Beggars, *anonymous painting. According to Sir Walter Scott, '"The Jolly Beggars", for humorous description and nice discrimination of character, is inferior to no poem of the same length in the whole range of English poetry'. Despite his mastery of monologue this cantata was the closest Burns came to drama. He contemplated dramatising the folk-tale of Omeron Cameron and there were plans for a play entitled 'Rob McQuechan's Elshon', but neither materialised.*

Burns is to be dissuaded from tethering in future:

> Tell him, if e'er again he keep
> As muckle gear as buy a sheep,
> O, bid him never tye them mair,
> Wi' wicked strings o' hemp or hair!
> But ca them out to park or hill,
> An' let them wander at their will:
> So, may his flock increase an' grow
> To scores o' lambs, and packs o' woo'.

Unfettered freedom will be good for the young sheep (avoiding Mailie's fate) and good for farmer Burns as they will mate more freely. However, when she turns from general principles to specific application to her own family she sounds a quite different note. Son is to be warned 'what I winna name,/ To stay content wi' yowes at hame', with the question, 'But will ye tell me, master Caesar,/ Sure great folk's life's a life o' pleasure?', Luath invites Caesar to explain in greater detail. In contrasting the neurosis, decadence, and pretension of the aristocracy, Caesar effectively endorses the peasantry's life of honest toil. That the ploughman's collie controls the outcome of the debate may reflect Burns's hopes for the future of Scotland.

'To a Mouse', like 'To a Mountain Daisy', was composed while the author was 'holding the plough', according to his brother Gilbert. From the first lines, 'Wee, sleeket, cowran, tim'rous beastie,/ O, what a panic's in thy breastie!', the speaker so empathises with the mouse as to distance himself from his fellow-mortals who have 'broken Nature's social union'. The breach in the natural harmony between human and natural worlds becomes metaphor for divisions amongst all created life, so that the mouse's homelessness can also represent human deprivation (his family's threatened eviction may have been in Burns's mind). So the speaker endows the mouse with human faculties:

But Mousie, thou art no thy-lane,
In proving foresight may be vain:
The best laid schemes o' Mice an' Men,
Gang aft agley,
An' lea'e us nought but grief an' pain,
For promis'd joy!

Fellow-victims of a hostile Providence, mouse and man fail to bring plans to fruition (Burns by this point having broken down the distinction between instinctive behaviour and rational insight). But in the final stanza the mouse is restored to its natural state: no longer capable of planning, it lives only in the present, consequently is 'blest' in comparison with the speaker who can brood over past failures and 'guess an' fear' as to what lies in store.

'To a Louse' also addresses a seemingly insignificant creature. This is a masterstroke of irony in that it is the despised creature that is truly free from the constraints of polite society and, unlike the speaker, can go where it pleases. In church the speaker's attention has been captured by the louse's attempt to ascend a young lady's bonnet, the implication being that he has been transfixed by her rather than heeding the sermon. From feigned affront at the creature's audacity the speaker moves to grudging admiration for its heroism and concern for its survival; it, after all, is where he would like to be. In the first two stanzas the speaker uses the expressive vernacular of the flyting tradition: 'Ha! where ye gaun, ye crowlan ferlie!/ Your impudence protects you sairly'; 'Ye ugly, creepan, blastet wonner,/ Detested, shunn'd by saunt an' sinner', and he tries to dispatch it to its natural habitat among the 'shoals and nations' of its kin on the head of the beggar.

O wad some Pow'r the giftie gie us To see oursels as others see us!

THE LANGUAGE OF BURNS

Burns is bilingual. For proof, compare his English prose account to Francis Grose of the genesis of 'Tam o' Shanter' and the language of the poem: 'he had got courageously drunk' becomes 'Tam had got planted unco right'. In the first two lines, 'When chapman billies leave the street,/ And drouthy neebors, neebors meet', he uses English, Scots-English, and Scots. Scots vernacular is especially suitable as a verbal weapon. The narrator reproduces Kate's 'flyting' of Tam: 'She tauld thee weel thou was a skellum,/ A blethering, blustering, drunken blellum'. Flyting originated as a duel with words between rival poets, a contest in vituperation staged as a Stuart court entertainment. Burns flytes the Devil in 'Address to the Deil'; in 'The Brigs of Ayr' the old and new bridges flyte each other; and in 'Address to the Toothache' the poet tries to flyte away his pain.

An' foolish notion:
What airs in dress an' gait wad lea'e us,
And ev'n Devotion!

Jenny is guilty of 'airs in dress'; both the louse and the high-flying Lunardi have been rising above their station (Lunardi was one of the first hot-air balloonists of the times, and fashionable ladies' bonnets were modelled on his balloon.). But who is guilty of 'airs in devotion'? It becomes evident that the satiric range of references includes the speaker himself: by offering his alternative sermon while in church he too has over-reached – the final exemplar of human vanity.

At an early stage Burns's talents as satirist drew an ambivalent response, as David Sillar, a contemporary of Burns, noted in his recollection of him in Tarbolton: 'His social disposition easily procured him acquaintance; but a certain satirical seasoning...while it set the rustic circle in a roar, was not unaccompanied by its kindred attendant – suspicious fear'. (Analogies might be drawn with audience reactions to alternative comedy: laughter is prompted by relief at escaping the attentions of the comedian combined with fear that one's turn will come.) David Sillar also commented, 'I recollect hearing his neighbours say that he had a great deal to say for himself, and that they suspected his principles. He wore the only tied hair in the parish; and in the church his plaid, which was of a particular colour, I think fillemot, he wrapped in a particular manner around his shoulders'. Charismatic, sociable, and gifted with what his friend Maria Riddell termed a 'sorcery' with words, Burns could draw a crowd. Yet his very talent marked him out within the crowd and, as Sillar's account suggests, he decided to play the part to the full, giving expression to his rebellious nature as well as his sense of social injustice. The 'satirical seasoning' came with a price. Maria Riddell later observed, 'the keenness of his satire [proved] a dangerous talent' and added, 'his wit...had always the start of his judgement'.

Burns Composing 'The Cotter's Saturday Night'
Gilbert gave this account of the poem's origins: 'Robert had frequently remarked to me that he thought there was something particularly venerable in the phrase, "Let us worship God!" used by a decent, sober head of a family, introducing family worship'. Robert recited the poem to him on a Sunday afternoon walk, 'one of those precious breathing times to the labouring part of the community'. Gilbert confirmed the cotter as 'an exact copy of my father'. However, the patriarch's emphasis on obedience to authority is at odds with his eldest son's extolling of independence.

Unsurprisingly deaf to his imprecations, the louse continues ever upwards, ignoring even his advice to shelter in the ribbons. After threatening the louse with insecticide or a kicking, the speaker reverts to astonishment at its disregard of social hierarchies: it might be expected to inhabit an old wife's flannel cap or an urchin's vest, 'But Miss's fine Lunardi, fye!/ How daur ye do't?'. The vanity of the young lady and that of the louse in not knowing its place are equated. From concern for the louse the speaker moves to concern for Jenny, now a comic figure to increasing numbers of the congregation. In the last stanza the speaker offers the thoughts that the episode has prompted:

O wad some Pow'r the giftie gie us
To see oursels as others see us!
It wad frae monie a blunder free us

Religion habitually had Burns sharpening his satirist's darts, especially Presbyterianism of the 'Auld Licht' (conservative) variety. In particular the notion that man was entitled to sit in judgement on his fellow-man riled him. Increasingly his own conduct made him an object of judgement. Elizabeth Paton, a farm-servant at Lochlie, gave birth to his daughter ('Dear-bought Bess') on 22 May 1785. Penance for fornication required the parents to appear before the congregation in Tarbolton kirk. In 'A Poet's Welcome to his Love-Begotten Daughter' (Burns also used the title 'Welcome to a Bastart Wean') he rings the emotional changes. A note of affectionate pride in addressing his first offspring gives way to a flying in the face of convention, almost a relishing of his further celebrity:

What tho' they ca' me fornicator,
An' tease my name in kintry clatter:
The mair they tauk I'm kent the better,
    E'en let them clash;
An auld wife's tongue's a feckless matter
    To gie ane fash.

He wore the badge with comparable defiance in 'The Fornicator. A New Song', and in 'The Rantin Dog the Daddie O't' the female speaker confidently asserts her rights, after penance, to further sexual fulfilment.

The Cottar's Saturday Night by Sir David Wilkie:
Burns's poem 'The Cotter's Saturday Night' prompted Mrs. Frances Dunlop (1730-1815) to write approvingly to Burns in autumn 1786. A lively correspondence developed in which they discussed subjects ranging from literature to matters of the heart. Burns sent drafts of poems and songs for her opinion, though he did not always abide by it; and she served as mother-confessor to him. He wrote more letters to her (77) than to anyone. However, she took exception to his referring to Louis XVI and Marie Antoinette as 'a perjured Blockhead and an unprincipled Prostitute' in a letter of 20 December 1794.

Dumfries 27th Dec: 1791

21

...have yours, my ever dearest Nancy, this moment. I have just ten minutes before the Post goes, & these shall employ in sending you some songs I have just been composing to different tunes for the Collection of songs, of which you have three volumes — & of which you shall have the fourth. —

Song — Tune, Rory Dall's port

Ae fond kiss, & then we sever;
Ae farewel, & then for ever!
Deep in heart-wrung tears I'll pledge thee,
Warring sighs & groans I'll wage thee. —

Wha shall say that Fortune grieves him
While the star of hope she leaves him?
Me, nae cheerful twinkle lights me;
Dark despair around benights me. —

I'll ne'er blame my partial fancy
Naething could resist my Nancy:
But to see her, was to love her,
Love but her, & love for ever. —

...nal Manuscript – ...ond Kiss':

...ong was the last, and ...the finest, of the ten ...inspired by the poet's ...nship with Mrs. Agnes ...y) McLehose. The ...ect of parting ...ularly stimulated Burns ...gsmith. He had briefly ...ancy again in ...urgh on 6 December ...and she confirmed her ...on of re-uniting with ...usband in Jamaica. ...weeks later Burns ...er this song from ...ries along with two ...(and inferior) songs of ...g. In January 1792 she ...l on the Roselle.

Also from this amazingly productive period is Burns's best-known satire, 'Holy Willie's Prayer', arguably the most forceful denunciation in world literature of the closed mind. Burns conceives of the prayer of William Fisher, elder of Mauchline parish, whose charges against Gavin Hamilton, lawyer friend of the poet, for offences against Sabbath observance had been dismissed by the Presbytery of Ayr. 'Holy Willie' unwittingly reveals the limitations of his 'Auld Licht' creed. Calvinist doctrine stresses that God predetermines the fate of each individual. Assured that he is one of the Elect, Willie praises God for the choice he has made. Why me? he wonders; he might as readily have been destined for eternal damnation, which is graphically rendered in the stock terms of the Evangelicals. Yet he is 'a chosen sample...a pillar in thy temple...A guide, a buckler, an example/ To a' thy flock'. Secure in this knowledge he admits to fornication 'wi' Meg', vowing 'I'll ne'er lift a lawless leg/ Again upon her' (the collision of the animalistic and the language of hell-fire sermon is particularly effective). Then he ventures even further in his confession but, far from standing by his sexual impulses, he uses the excuse of drunkenness: 'But, Lord, that Friday I was fou,/ When I cam near her,/ Or else, thou kens, thy servant true/ Wad never steer her'. Next he speculates as to why he is allowed to stray from the paths of righteousness:

It was probably the birth of Bess that induced him to write 'Address to the Unco Guid, or the Rigidly Righteous'. This poem exemplifies Burns's deflation of pretensions by undermining formality with vernacular Scots:

Ye high, exalted, virtuous Dames,
Ty'd up in godly laces,
Before ye gie poor Frailty names,
 Suppose a change o' cases;
A dear-lov'd lad, convenience snug,
A treacherous inclination –
But, let me whisper in your lug,
 Ye're aiblens nae temptation.

Its final stanza expresses two ideas central to Burns's thinking: judgement is the right of God alone; and the only true morality is the morality of the heart.

Maybe thou lets this fleshly thorn
Buffet thy servant e'en and morn,
Lest he owre proud and high should turn
That he's sae gifted:
If sae, thy han' maun e'en be borne
Until thou lift it.

His creed's emphasis on predetermination justifies his continuing to endure the pleasures of the flesh: the onus is with his God, to whom he can boast of his exploits in locker-room fashion. In invoking vengeance on the liberals, Willie reveals the limitations of his theology: 'Curse thou his basket and his store,/ Kail and potatoes'. The Auld Lichts can respond to the challenge of enlightened thought only in physical terms of a most negative kind: Willie still quakes at the thought of 'how we stood, sweatin', shakin',/ And pissed wi' dread'. Their humiliation explains the ferocity of his call to God to destroy his enemies 'for thy people's sake'. Willie then changes his tone for his final petition, striking a bargain with God:

> But Lord remember me and mine
> Wi' mercies temporal and divine,
> That I for gear and grace may shine,
> Excell'd by nane,
> An' a' the glory shall be thine,
> Amen, Amen.

The alliterating twins, 'gear and grace', say it all: self-interest has masqueraded as religious devotion, ironically using the form and terminology of the prayer. Burns, true to his principles, declines to pass judgement; sublimely detached, he has enabled Holy Willie to condemn himself unwittingly from his own mouth. In revealing the limitations of the closed mind Burns produces one of the great texts of the Scottish Enlightenment.

Burns, as a humane advocate of progress, challenges the hold which superstition and religion exercise over the mind of the people. 'Death and Dr. Hornbook' offers another role-reversal: the drunken but benign peasant offers a sympathetic ear to Death, threatened with redundancy by the efforts of the amateur apothecary (inspired by the Tarbolton schoolmaster, John Wilson, who advertised remedies). What is to be feared is not Death, Burns makes plain, but the corruption of those who rely on Hornbook's incompetence to further their evil plans. Likewise, in 'Address to the Deil' the awesome figure of the epigraph from Milton's 'Paradise Lost' is humanised into a member of the local community and

SUPERSTITION IN BURNS'S TIME

Superstition was still rife, especially in rural areas. When a bull became trapped in the old kirk of Alloway, its bellowing and a glimpse of its horns convinced a woman she had seen the Devil. First published in 1685, George Sinclair's *Satan's Invisible World Discovered* ran through several editions and remained popular into the 19th century (Sir Walter Scott designated it 'the darling of the Scottish vulgar'). In 'Address to the Deil' Burns cites his 'rev'rend Graunie' as the source of legends regarding the haunts and ploys of the Devil. On one level Burns tries to entertain the locals, but his humanising the Devil and witches (as in 'Tam o' Shanter') is consistent with the secularising of the Scottish Enlightenment. In a letter he adopts his grannie's 'classic phrase, SPUNKIE [will-o'-the-wisp]' on which he claims the Devil rides, as his 'Symbol, Signature, & Tutelary Genius': and typically, he uses the term as synonym for whisky.

Burns, radically challenging orthodox Presbyterianism, ends with offering to 'auld Nickie-ben' the possibility of reform, since even the Devil does not deserve eternal torment.

Alloway Kirk from the West by John Fleming: Alloway Kirk had ceased use as a place of worship in 1691.

Romantic Complications and Literary Triumphs

Ever responsive to literature, Burns found models in it for his conduct. In the song, 'O leave novels, ye Mauchline belles' he warns the young ladies that 'Such witching books, are baited hooks/ For rakish rooks like Rob Mossgiel'. In Fielding's Tom Jones, specifically mentioned, he found a literary precedent for his amorousness, candidly admitting, 'That feeling heart but acts a part,/ 'Tis rakish art in Rob Mossgiel...The frank address and politesse/ Are all finesse in Rob Mossgiel'. As one of 'the ram-stam boys, the rattling squad', Burns founded 'The Court of Equity' with his friends John Richmond, James Smith, and William Hunter. They met in the Whitefoord Arms Inn, Mauchline, in a burlesque of the kirk session, to call to account, for their fornication, the young men of the village. ('Libel Summons' records the proceedings').

The circumstances of Burns's first encounter with Jean Armour were not auspicious. When she pelted his dog for running on to her washing he retorted. 'Lassie, if ye thought ought o' me ye wadna hurt my dog'. Jean's reaction was, 'I wadna think much o' you at onie rate'. Soon, though, she took pride of place among 'The Belles of Mauchline': 'Armour's the jewel for me o' them a''. Romance flourished despite the opposition of her father, James Armour. When Jean fell pregnant Burns gave her a document of attestation, a form of civil wedding in Scotland. Her father had the lawyer, Robert Aiken, cut their names from the document, annulling the marriage; and he despatched Jean to relatives in Paisley. Robert Wilson, a young weaver, was encouraged to court her there, though Jean later denied that she showed any interest.

Burns's response in a letter to Gavin Hamilton, 15 April 1786, reveals his intense mix of emotions: 'Perdition seize her falsehood, and perjurious perfidy! but God bless her and forgive my poor, once-dear, misguided girl. She is ill-advised. Do not despise me, Sir: I am indeed a fool, but a *knave* is an infinitely worse character than anybody, I hope, will dare to give the unfortunate Robt. Burns'; and in other letters of the time he inveighs against one of his arch-enemies, Prudence. Returning to Mauchline on 9 June, Jean reported her pregnancy to the kirk session. Two weeks later Burns appeared before them and admitted fornication. Rebuked on three successive Sundays, but spared the humiliation of the 'cutty stool', he was granted a certificate of bachelorhood by Reverend Auld.

On 22 July 1786 Burns transferred his share of Mossgiel to Gilbert by Deed of Assignment, and went underground to evade the imprisonment that Armour's writ threatened. From Old Rome Foord he wrote, 'For me, I am witless wild, and wicked; and have scarcely any vestige of the image of God left me, except a pretty large portion of honour and an enthusiastic, incoherent Benevolence. If you see Jean tell her, I will meet her'. Jean was by now eight months pregnant, but Burns's personal life had taken another twist. He had met Mary (or Margaret) Campbell, a native of Argyll, a nursemaid in Gavin Hamilton's house in

Portrait of Burns (1786) by Peter Taylor:
Peter Taylor (1756-88) was a sign-writer and coach-painter. His portrait of Burns, in oils on wood, has the distinction of being the earliest. It is also the least romanticised representation of the poet. Possibly for that reason, it was thought by some to be of Gilbert rather than Robert. In 1828 Mrs. McLehose wrote, 'In my opinion it is the most striking likeness of the poet I have ever seen; and I say this with much confidence, having a perfect recollection of his appearance'.

Robert Burns & Highland Mary by Thomas Faed:
Burns's relationship with 'Highland Mary' Campbell has a romantic aura in excess of what is factually known. According to Burns's mother and sister, the poet turned his attention to Mary Campbell after Jean Armour had been packed off to Paisley relatives by her enraged father.

17

Mauchline, and later dairymaid at Coilsfield, home of Col. Hugh Montgomerie. The short affair culminated in mid-May 1786 in their exchanging Bibles as token of eternal love. If 'Will ye go the the Indies, my Mary?' is to be read biographically, their parting was prelude to her returning to join him in emigration.

BURNS AND THE KIRK

Burns once wrote, 'I used to puzzle Calvinism with so much heat and indiscretion that I raised a hue and cry of heresy against me which has not ceased to this hour'. His sympathies were with the New Licht (liberal) faction in the church. When Dr William McGill became a target of Auld Licht (conservatives) censure, Burns threatened, 'I shall keep no measure with the savages, but fly at them with the faulcons of Ridicule, or run them down with the bloodhounds of Satire'. In poems and letters Burns testified to 'the Religion of the Heart'. His devotion to it unleashed 'the houghmagandie pack' on him and he had to do penance. The clergy were a pet target: Burns claimed to be breeding his son Robert for the church because of his 'innate dexterity in secret Mischief...and a certain hypocritical gravity as he looks on the consequences'.

Certainly 'Highland Mary' inspired later songs such as 'The Highland Lassie, O'; 'Afton Water' ('My Mary's asleep by thy murmuring stream'); the poignant 'Thou Lingering Star', composed around the third anniversary of her death; and 'Highland Mary'. Oddly, when Burns sent 'Will ye go to the Indies, my Mary?' to George Thomson (editor of the *Select Collection of Scottish Airs*) in October 1792 he was dismissive: 'In my very early years, when I was thinking of going to the West Indies, I took the following farewell of a dear girl...It is quite trifling...but it will fill up this page'.

The issue of Burns's proposed emigration is also controversial, with some scholars questioning the seriousness of his intentions. It seems likely that for a time it offered an escape-route. In April 1786 he wrote, 'Already the holy beagles, the houghmagandie pack, begin to sniff the scent...but as I am an old fox...I intend to earth among the mountains of Jamaica'. It is likely that the overblown 'The Farewell. To the Brethren of St. James's Lodge, Tarbolton' was composed for a masonic meeting on 24 June. On 30 July Burns wrote to John Richmond from Old Rome Foord, 'My hour is come. You and I will never meet in Britain more'. Detailing ship, route, and departure-date he adds, 'This, except to our friend Smith...is a secret about Mauchline', and he denounces the behaviour of Armour that has necessitated his leaving. Two weeks on, having apparently accepted Charles Douglas's offer of a clerkship on his plantation, he notified James Smith that his plans were 'deranged' by the discovery that the ship would land him on the wrong side of Jamaica. On 1 September he claimed that the ship had left too soon for him and gave a revised departure at the end of the month, but added 'I am under little apprehension now about Armour. The warrant is still in existence, but some of the first Gentlemen in the county have offered to befriend me; and besides, Jean will not take steps against me without letting me know, as nothing but the most violent menaces could have forced her to sign the Petition'.

On 3 September 1786 Jean gave birth to twins, baptized Robert and Jean by Rev. Auld two days later. On the day of their birth Burns sent John Richmond a stanza of 'Green grow the Rashes' with the comment, 'Armour has just now brought me a fine boy and girl at one throw'. By 26 September he was waxing lyrical in a letter about 'the burning glow when [man] clasps the Woman of his Soul to his bosom – the tender yearnings of heart for the little Angels to whom he has given existence', and he adds, 'My departure is uncertain, but I do not think it will be till after harvest'.

A combination of circumstances decided matters for Burns. One was the publication of *Poems, chiefly in the Scottish Dialect*. Burns had sent proposals for publishing to John Wilson and subscription-notices appeared on 17 April 1786. From receipt of the poems in mid-June, Wilson completed in six weeks the printing of 612 copies for sale at three shillings each. By 27 September 1786 Burns indicated that, but for the cost of paper, he would authorise a second edition. Dr. George Lawrie, minister of Loudoun parish, had sent a copy of the Kilmarnock edition to Dr. Thomas Blacklock in Edinburgh. His favourable response in a letter of 4 September led Burns to visit the Lawrie household in early October with the two-fold effect of showing him a model of family life and encouraging him to try his literary fortune in the capital. Simultaneous news of the death of Mary Campbell removed any lingering personal obligations there.

Before leaving this period in Burns's life it is worth recognising the psychological significance of his increasing tendency to identify procreation and poetic creativity. In a letter of 12 June 1786 they are juxtaposed: 'The ship is on her way home that is to take me out to Jamaica, and then, farewell dear old Scotland, and farewell dear, ungrateful Jean, for never, never, will I see you more! You will have heard that I am going to commence Poet in print; and tomorrow, my works go to the press'. Sending a song in October 1787, he writes, 'The inclosed is one which, like some other misbegotten

brats, too tedious to mention, claims a parental pang from my Bardship'. Most telling of all is this, written September 1794: 'Making a poem is like begetting a son: you cannot know whether you have a wise man or a fool, until you produce him to the world and try him. For that reason I send you the offspring of my brain, abortions and all'.

BURNS AND DRINK

Burns celebrated alcohol and the conviviality it induced. 'FREEDOM and WHISKY gang thegither', he wrote in 'The Author's Earnest Cry'; and in a letter he claimed, 'a universal Philanthropist [is] A BOTTLE OF GOOD OLD PORT'. Two poems offer contrasting views of drink's effects: 'oil'd by thee,/The wheels o' life gae down-hill, scrievin,/ Wi' rattlin glee' ('Scotch Drink'); 'Satan, I fear thy sooty claws,/ I hate thy brunstane stink,/ And ay I curse the luckless cause - / The wicked soup o' drink' ('Epistle to William Stewart'). Hungover, he found 'one comfort': 'I suffer so much...in this world, for last night's debauch, that I shall escape scot-free for it in the world to come'. No alcoholic, he conceded, 'it is the private parties...among the hard drinking gentlemen of this country that do me the mischief'. In his account of a roup at Ellisland he noted that even his dogs had become intoxicated from drinking the spillage.

Burns's poem 'The Whi[...] immortalises a drinking contest held in Octobe[r] 1789, when the victor downed eight bottles o[f] claret. The prize was a[n] ancient ebony whistle brought from Denmar[k]

Edinburgh, the Tours and Edinburgh again

On 27 November 1786 on a borrowed pony Burns set out for Edinburgh with hopes of a second edition and a career in the Excise. Already renowned, he was warmly received by the communities en route. In Edinburgh he took lodgings with his old Mauchline friend John Richmond, a lawyer's clerk.

Burns's reputation preceded him and he was feted. Sir James Hunter Blair, the Lord Provost, hosted a reception for him; he was feted by Jane, Duchess of Gordon; and James, Earl of Glencairn, became his patron. He later wrote: 'At Edinburgh I was in a new world'.

The literati greeted Burns with adulation: Dugald Stewart arranged for publication in *The Lounger*; James Sibbald reviewed favourably in his *Edinburgh Magazine*; and in *The Lounger* Henry Mackenzie enthused over 'this Heaven-taught Ploughman' in a review which reflected the tastes of the cultured circles: he praised poems of sensibility such as 'To a Mountain Daisy' and discouraged writing in vernacular Scots. Far from being 'Heaven-taught', Burns was widely and deeply read, but he was happy to collude in the deception. Scotland needed a great writer to match England in cultural terms. If, proving Scotland's responsiveness to the vogue of sensibility, he could be projected as both Man of Feeling and Noble Savage as Poet so much the better. By 1 December 1786 Burns was writing as a 'bard of Nature's making'.

Burns's circle of friends widened. In Dowie's tavern he drank with William Nicol and Allan Masterton, masters in the High School; and William Smellie, printer of his poems and editor and printer of the first *Encyclopaedia Britannica*, introduced him to the Crochallan Fencibles, a convivial group for whom Burns collected many of the bawdy ballads that comprised *The Merry Muses of Caledonia* (James Currie, Burns's first editor, added a note, as if by Burns, 'A very few are my own'). In Edinburgh Burns formed a strong attraction to Margaret Chalmers, a relative of Gavin Hamilton, and wrote two songs for her. Later she claimed that she had rejected his proposal.

Despite the euphoria of Edinburgh, Burns felt insecure there, a fact reflected in the frequency of letters to Ayrshire friends. He wrote to Gavin Hamilton, 7 December 1786, 'I am in a fair way of becoming as eminent as Thomas a Kempis or John Bunyan; and you may expect henceforth to see my birthday inserted among the wonderful events in...the Almanacks'. On 13 January 1787 he was toasted as 'Caledonia's Bard' by the Grand Lodge of Scotland. Yet Burns increasingly felt the burden of celebrity and predicted that his meteoric rise would herald an equally rapid fall. He confided on 16 December 1786, 'Various concurring circumstances have raised my fame as a Poet to a height which I am absolutely certain I have not merits to support; and I look down on the future as I would into the bottomless pit'. By 4 March 1789 he was complaining, 'My success has encouraged such a shoal of ill-spawned monsters to crawl into public notice under the title of Scots Poets, that the very term, Scots Poetry, borders on the burlesque'. Herein lay one reason for devoting his energies to song-writing and song-collecting.

Burns had an ambivalent attitude to the guidance offered by Edinburgh intellectuals: though welcoming support he was determined to remain his own man. To Mrs. Dunlop he wrote, 22 March 1787, 'I have the advice of some very judicious friends among the Literati here, but with them I sometimes find it necessary to claim the privilege of thinking for myself'.

Burns's rebellious nature combined with a sense of alienation from his roots to lead to identification with 'a very respectable Personage, Milton's Satan' as he wrote in a letter to Mrs. Dunlop of 30 April 1787. Milton's Satan became a personal icon, being variously referred to in letters to Smith, 11 June 1787 ('Give me a spirit like my favourite hero, Milton's Satan'); to Nicol, 18 June 1787 ('...the desperate daring and noble defiance of hardship in that great Personage, Satan'); and to Mrs. Riddell, 1 June 1796 ('I may...rejoice with the rejoicing of an Apostate Angel'). Most revealing in terms of Burns's personal psychology and his chameleon tendencies is this to Cunningham, 8 August 1790: 'The resemblance that hits my fancy best is, that poor, blackguard Miscreant, Satan, who, as Holy Writ tells us, roams about like a roaring lion, seeking, *searching*, whom he may devour'.

Burns found relief from the hothouse atmosphere of Edinburgh in a series of tours which furthered the process of song-collecting and heightened his awareness of Scottish history. On 6 May 1787 he left to tour the Borders, accompanied initially by his lawyer friend, Robert Ainslie. They briefly crossed into England on 7 May and Burns was said to have kissed the Scottish soil on returning over the Coldstream bridge. They visited Kelso, Roxburgh, Jedburgh, Dryburgh Abbey, and Melrose, where the heart of Robert the Bruce lay, and Ercildoune of Thomas the Rhymer fame.

Burns in Edinburgh (1787) after C. M. Hardie: In Edinburgh Burns mixed with all classes. His first lodging was in the old town, in Baxter's Close, Lawnmarket. His landlady, Mrs. Carfrae, had problem neighbours, as he indicated in a letter of 14 January 1787: 'My landlady...is a staid, sober, piously disposed, skulldudery-abhoring Widow...She is at present in sore tribulation respecting some "Daughters of Belial" who are on the floor immediately above'. In fashionable society, Henry Mackenzie's The Man of Feeling was read aloud in the salons and the company would weep openly, proving their sensibility and moral worth. Early in 1783 Burns described the text as 'a book I prize next to the Bible' and 'one of the glorious models after which I endeavour to form my conduct'.

O my Luve's like a red, red rose...

Again venturing south, Burns viewed the castles of Alnwick, Warkworth, and Morpeth. His visit to Carlisle proved eventful: a girl, accompanied by her married sister, offered him 'a Gretna Green affair'; and he was brought before the mayor for allowing his horse to graze on municipal ground, but the case was dropped for fear of his skill in lampooning.

From Carlisle, 1 June ('or I believe the 39th o' May rather') Burns sent his friend William Nicol a letter entirely in Scots (his only such example). At Dumfries he was made an Honorary Burgess and visited Patrick Miller at Dalswinton to discuss farms. On 2 June he received a letter from May (Peggy) Cameron, an Edinburgh servant-girl, alleging she was pregnant by him. He sent money to her, but it seems likely she miscarried, since Burns was freed from her writ on 15 August. Returning briefly to Ayrshire, he visited Mossgiel and, welcomed by the Armours, was reunited with Jean, and, as he later wrote to Mrs. Dunlop, 'the usual consequences began to betray her'.

From Glasgow Burns embarked on a short tour of the West Highlands with Dr. George Grierson. Highlights, as recounted vividly in a letter of 30 June 1787 to James Smith, were an all-night party when, the ladies having retired at 3a.m., the gentlemen went to 'pay our devotions to the glorious lamp of day peering over the towering top of Ben Lomond', and a frantic lochside horse-race with a Highlander that ended in collision. On 25 August Burns left Edinburgh in a chaise to tour the Highlands with William Nicol, their route showing Burns the Scotland of history (Linlithgow, Bannockburn, Ossian's grave, Culloden, Scone) and the new industrialising Scotland at Carron Ironworks.

Back in Edinburgh, Burns wrote a letter to his brother Gilbert on 17 September 1787, 'after a tour of 22 days, and travelling near 600 miles'. On 4 October he was off again, making a brief tour of Stirlingshire with Dr. James Adair.

These travels bore a rich harvest of songs, some composed, others collected, and yet others where he wrote words to existing airs. In particular, the pathos of the Jacobite fate struck a chord with a sensibility always inclined to empathise with victims; hence the moving 'Lament of Mary Queen of Scots'. 'Here Stewarts once in Triumph Reigned' he inscribed on an inn window in Stirling. Its publication in the *Edinburgh Courant*, 5 October 1787, almost jeopardised his chances of an excise post, and he returned and smashed the window. It is possible that Burns projected the sense of displacement which he now felt in both Edinburgh and Ayrshire – starkly represented in a letter to William Nicol from Mauchline, 18 June 1787 – on to the exiled Stuart Prince:

Tho' somehing like moisture conglobes in my eye,
Let no man misdeem me disloyal;
A poor, friendless wand'rer may well claim a sigh
Still more if that Wand'rer were royal.

Burns was undeniably a nationalist from childhood when, as he wrote, 'the story of Wallace poured a Scottish prejudice in my veins which will boil along there till the flood-gates of life shut in eternal rest'. 'Such a Parcel of Rogues in a Nation' and other songs convey deep regret at the loss of independence and, like his contemporaries, Burns could wax nostalgic about what might have been. Also, there is abundant evidence of his distaste for the manipulation of the masses by the few, something he believed increased under the Hanoverians. But it is difficult to argue that these factors combine to constitute a belief in the restoration of the Stuarts. Primarily Burns was a cultural nationalist: 'The appelation of a Scotch Bard is by far my highest pride; to continue to deserve it is my most exalted ambition. Scottish scenes, and Scottish story are the themes I could wish to sing', he told Mrs. Dunlop on 22 March 1787. Arguably, his contribution to sustaining an element of Scottish independence lies in the preservation of the song-culture.

In October 1787 Burns was back in Edinburgh collating material for James Johnson's *Scots Musical Museum*. He had his silhouette done in profile by John Miers. Delighted with it, he had it reproduced in miniature as both jewelry and card reproduction. In late October he assured his friend Margaret Chalmers, 'I hate dissimulation in the language of the heart',

while in the same letter lamenting, 'My rhetoric seems quite to have lost its effect on the lovely half of mankind'. Both these claims were contradicted by his next amorous adventure. On 4 December 1787 Burns met Mrs. Agnes (Nancy) McLehose, a few months his elder and mother of three children, her husband already some years ensconced in Jamaica. Burns injured his knee in a fall from a coach, and it was 4 January 1788 before they again met. Over fourteen weeks they conducted a love-affair by letters, highly stylised and overwrought, using the pastoral pseudonyms 'Sylvander' and 'Clarinda'. She was plainly smitten from the first encounter, whereas Burns relished the role of Henry Mackenzie's 'Man of Feeling' in love, though after their reunion he seems to have become more involved emotionally. However her religious and social scruples kept the affair Platonic and the only consummation was on paper in their exchange of poems and songs. Burns fathered a child by her maid, Jenny Clow, who died of tuberculosis in January 1792, though the son, Robert Burns, thrived and became a successful merchant.

The poems and songs inspired by the affair, such as 'Clarinda, Mistress of My Soul' and 'To Clarinda, with a present of a pair of drinking glasses' are undistinguished to say the least. But their parting on 6 December 1791 when she rejoined her husband (not for long, as it transpired) drew from Burns the deeply moving 'Ae Fond Kiss'. For Sir Walter Scott, stanza 4 of this song was 'the essence of a thousand love tales'. Burns later referred to Nancy pretentiously in a letter of 19 October 1794, as 'a ci-devant Goddess of mine'; and to the copy of his penultimate letter to her, found in the Glenriddell Manuscripts, in which he again raved amorously, he added, 'I need scarcely remark that the foregoing was the fustian rant of enthusiastic youth'. In marked contrast, Nancy McLehose's diary entry for 6 December 1831 reads, 'This day I can never forget. Parted with Burns in the year 1791, never more to meet in this world. Oh, may we meet in Heaven!'.

Mrs. Agnes McLehose & Her House at 14 Calton Hill:
Agnes McLehose (1759-1841) was the daughter of Andrew Craig, a Glasgow surgeon. James McLehose, a young law agent of whom her family disapproved, succeeded in his courtship by purchasing all the seats on the Glasgow-Edinburgh coach in which he knew she would travel. At 17 she married him and gave birth to four children in four years (one died in infancy). Leaving a turbulent marriage she returned to her father, but when he died in 1782 she moved to an apartment in General's Entry, Potter Row. She supported her children with an annuity and help from her uncle William (later Lord) Craig, a Judge of Session. Both he and her minister, Reverend John Kemp of Tolbooth Church, deplored the effect on her reputation of her involvement with Burns. The illustration shows her residence in later years.

Ellisland, Marriage, Dumfries and the Excise

Burns inspected Ellisland farm in late February 1788 and was advised by family friend John Tennant of Glenconner to take it. Earlier that month he had asked James Cunningham, Earl of Glencairn, to support his Excise candidacy. So in effect he was keeping his options open. In personal relations, too, Burns was a man of many parts. As 'Sylvander' he informed 'Clarinda' from Mossgiel, 'Now for a little news that will please you. I, this morning as I came home, called for a certain woman. I am disgusted with her; I cannot endure her!'. This was Jean, heavily pregnant with twins, to whom she gave birth on 10 March (both died, one at birth, the other twelve days later). Burns meantime was again in Edinburgh, trying to settle a financial dispute with his publisher William Creech, and visiting 'Clarinda'. Back in Ayrshire from late March, he took instruction in the Excise and on 2 May was married to Jean in a civil ceremony in Hamilton's office.

Burns's references to the marriage are characteristically motley. In several letters he develops the metaphor of Jean's being put on trial, judged, and found not guilty. To Robert Ainslie he boasted, 'I have been extremely fortunate in all my buyings and bargainings hitherto; Mrs. Burns not excepted, which title I now avow to the world'. He delayed telling Mrs. Dunlop for a month, and when she questioned their compatibility he assured her that he loved Jean 'near to distraction' and added, 'circumstanced as I am, I could never have got a female Partner for life who could have entered into my favorite studies'. (Jean was reported to have said on one occasion, 'Robert should hae had twa wives'.) On 9 September 1788 he commended the matrimonial state: 'I can speak from Experience; tho' God knows, my choice was as random as Blind-man's buff'. Yet three days later he wrote to Jean from Ellisland, 'My dear Love, I received your kind letter with a pleasure which no letter but one from you could have given me', and the sincerity contrasts markedly with the posturing to 'Clarinda'. The songs which Jean inspired – 'I Love My Jean' ('Of a' the airts the wind can blaw') and 'O, were I on Parnassus Hill' – bear the hallmarks of genuine emotion.

After Edinburgh, which had confirmed his Bardic image, Burns had an increasing awareness, reflected in his letters, of his multiple identity. He moved to Ellisland as Bard, farmer, husband, father, and potential exciseman. The stresses of his last years were psychological as well as physical. Burns leased the 170-acres of Ellisland from Patrick Miller from Whitsunday 1788 at a rent of £50 per annum. While the farmhouse was being built he lodged in conditions hazardous to his health. To Margaret Chalmers he wrote, 16 September 1788, 'This hovel that I shelter in...is pervious to every blast that blows, and every shower that falls; and I am only preserved from being chilled to death, by being suffocated with smoke'.

Burns described himself in a letter to

him in rented rooms in the Isle, the country house of Dumfries lawyer, David Newall; and in June 1789 they moved into Ellisland, a maid preceding them bearing, as token of good luck, a bowl of salt and the family Bible. The family increased with the birth on 18 August 1789 of Francis Wallace (died 1803), named in tribute to his godmother, Mrs. Dunlop. On 31 March 1791 Helen Anne Park, barmaid in the Globe Inn, gave birth to Burns's daughter, Elizabeth. Jean raised the child along with her son, William Nicol Burns (1791-1872), born ten days later. Jean gave birth to another daughter, Elizabeth Riddell Burns, on 21 November 1792, but she died in September 1795.

Burns's neighbour at Ellisland was Captain Robert Riddell, a keen antiquarian. He made available to Burns the Hermitage, a summer-house on his premises, Friars Carse. Together they founded the Monkland Friendly Society and built up its library, and Burns wrote an account of the Society for Sir John Sinclair's *Statistical Account of Scotland*. Burns had always made copies of those of his letters which especially pleased him, and on 27 April 1791 he presented a collection to Riddell (subsequently known as the Glenriddell Manuscripts). Burns found the Riddells most convivial. Their friend, Deborah Duff Davies he celebrated in the song 'Bonie Wee Thing', and at Friars Carse he met Francis Grose, the antiquarian, to whose *Antiquities of Scotland* he contributed 'Tam o' Shanter'.

An unfortunate incident caused a breach in relations with the Riddell family. After a dinner at Friars Carse the topic of the rape of the Sabine women in Roman times was discussed by the men, who proposed re-enacting the scene. When the ladies joined them it was only Burns who participated, eagerly seizing an alarmed Maria Riddell, Robert's sister-in-law. A remorseful Burns wrote an apology 'from the regions of Hell, amid the horrors of the damned' and claimed as excuse 'the heat of a fever of intoxication'. He paid the price of the loss of the friendship of Robert and

Robert Ainslie of 30 June 1788 as 'only a sojourner in a strange land in this place'; and in 'Epistle to Hugh Parker' he wryly sketched his situation, 'Wi' nae converse but Gallowa' bodies,/ Wi' nae kend face but Jenny Geddes' (his mare). To John Tennant he recommended moving to the area and resuming distilling since 'the Whisky of this country is a most rascally liquor; and by consequence, only drunk by the most rascally part of the inhabitants'.

In August 1788 Burns and Jean had their marriage recognised by the Mauchline kirk session, Burns paying a guinea to the poor as penalty. In December Jean joined

Elizabeth Riddell, and it was December 1794 before Maria resumed her friendship with him.

By March 1789 Creech had settled with Burns. Of the £450 Burns gave £200 to Gilbert to help support the family at Mossgiel. Ellisland, he told Mrs. Dunlop in the same letter of 25 March, had proved 'a very, very hard bargain, if at all practicable'. By 11 January 1790 he was writing to Gilbert, 'My nerves are in a damnable state. I feel that horrid hypochondria pervading every atom of both body and soul. This farm has undone my enjoyment of myself' - that last sentence is especially revealing psychologically. In August 1791 Burns sold the lease back to Miller and auctioned his crops.

In November the family moved to a first-floor flat in Bank Street (then known as the Stinking Vennel) in Dumfries. There they remained until 19 May 1793 when they moved to a house in Mill Hole Brae (now Burns Street). Burns had been an exciseman since 1 September 1789. During the first winter he rode many miles in the course of his duties, beneficial in that he composed while 'jogging home', but debilitating also.

In July 1790 Burns was promoted to the Dumfries Third Division, involving local duties on foot. Further promotion to the Port Division in 1792 saw his salary rise to £70 per year plus gratuities. From December 1794 to April 1795 he was Acting Supervisor when Alexander Findlater was ill. The winter of 1795 was particularly severe. On duty in Ecclefechan, Burns was trapped by snowdrifts ten feet deep. He wrote to George Thomson, 7 February 1795, 'To add to my misfortune; since dinner, a Scraper has been torturing Catgut, in sounds that would have insulted the dying agonies of a Sow under the hands of a Butcher...I have been in a dilemma, either to get drunk, to forget these miseries; or to hang myself, to get rid of these miseries'. He opted for the former.

A dramatic event of February 1792 has been cited as evidence of Burns's political sympathies. A brig, the 'Rosamond', was seized on suspicion of smuggling at Sarkfoot on the Solway by excisemen, including Burns, and dragoons. Tradition has it that Burns purchased at the auction of the ship's contents four carronades which he sent to the French revolutionaries, but no document corroborating the purchase exists. He was, however, suspected of Reformist sympathies. At the Theatre Royal, Dumfries, on 28 October 1792 a call for the national anthem was countered by republican sympathisers demanding the revolutionary chant, 'Ca ira'. It was alleged that Burns remained silent and wore his hat throughout the national anthem. In a letter

Globe Close & Globe Inn, Dumfries, after Allan Cunningham: Burns wrote in 1796 referring to 'the Globe Tavern here, which for these many years has been my HOWFF'. In June 1790 Burns had an affair with landlord William Hyslop's second cousin, Helen Anne Park, barmaid in 'The Globe'. 'Anna of the gowden locks', she inspired the love-song he judged his finest, 'Yestreen, I had a pint of wine'.

to Mrs. Dunlop of 6 December he reported
the incident and added, 'For me, I am a
Placeman, you know; a very humble one
indeed, heaven knows, but still so much so
as to gag me from joining in the cry. What
my private sentiments are, you will find out
without an Interpreter'. Reported to the
Excise Board as 'disaffected', by 31
December he had word of an official
enquiry into his politics. On 5 January 1793
Burns wrote at length in his defence to
Graham of Fintry, a commissioner of the
Scottish board of excise. The outcome of
the enquiry was to caution Burns and advise

him to be prudent in his political
statements. It seems that he was more
circumspect if this written in February 1794
is representative: 'The country, at least in
our part of it, is still progressive to the
devil. For my part, 'I jouk & let the jaw flee
o'er". Yet his natural sympathies were
always with the individual against the state,
the oppressed against the oppressor. Liberty
was a cause always close to his heart. In
Gatehouse on 1 August 1793 he witnessed
the radical lawyer, Thomas Muir of
Huntershill, a leading member of The
Friends of the People, being taken in chains
to Edinburgh to be tried for sedition. In late
August 1793 he sent the most patriotic of
his songs, 'Scots Wha Hae' ('Robert Bruce's
March to Bannockburn') to George
Thomson. Burns wrote, 'I had no idea of
giving myself any trouble on the subject, till
the accidental recollection of that glorious
struggle for Freedom, associated with the
glowing ideas of some other struggles of the
same nature, *not quite so ancient*, roused my
rhyming mania'. The reference may be to
America or France, but it is significant that
the letter coincides with the start of the trial
of Muir, advocate of both parliamentary
reform and Scottish independence.

Burns's 'A Man's a Man for a' that', a

The Haggis Feast by Alexander Carse:
The poet's widow recalled their domestic life in Dumfries: 'Burns was not an early riser, excepting when he had something particular to do in the way of his profession...The family breakfasted at nine. If he lay long in bed awake, he was always reading. At all meals he had a book beside him at the table. He did his work in the forenoon and was seldom engaged professionally in the evening. Dined at two o'clock when he dined at home. Was fond of plain things, and hated tarts, pies, and puddings'. During the 1830s his son Robert described life at Mill Street: 'There was much rough comfort in the house...for the poet received many presents of jam and country produce from the rural gentlefolk, besides occasional barrels of oysters from Hill, Cunningham, and other friends in town; so that [Burns] possibly was as much envied by some of his neighbours as he has since been pitied by the general body of his countrymen'.

'TO A HAGGIS'

Now a highlight of Burns suppers, this poem was recited by the poet at dinner-parties in Mauchline and Edinburgh. It is a masterpiece of comic exaggeration, with the mock-heroic element evident from the start when the speaker wishes that good fortune may befall the huge creature that is about to be sliced open and consumed. Burns, like Ramsay and Fergusson, ingeniously finds metaphors for nationalism. A national dish is used to represent and celebrate Scottish qualities, in contrast with those of the French. The health of a nation is dependent on its food, the speaker implies, and he sees good Scots fare as the source of Scots virility and heroism. Superficially comic and chauvinist, the poem may, on another level, be a rallying cry to the nation. In Burns's day haggis comprised grated liver and entrails blended with suet, spices and onions all boiled in a sheep's stomach. Ironically, Burns, as Jean Armour later testfied, 'hated' fatty sausages and puddings.

poetic equivalent of Tom Paine's *The Rights of Man*, has become a universal anthem of humankind. The influence of Adam Smith's *Theory of Moral Sentiments* is also evident: it is 'the man o' independent mind', unimpressed by wealth or status, who represents Burns's hope that 'Sense and worth, o'er a' the earth/ Shall bear the gree, an a' that'.

Burns's masterpiece, 'Tam o' Shanter' is perhaps the most subtly radical of his poems. Its epigraph from Gavin Douglas's

Eneados (1513) locates it within the Scottish literary tradition; by using features of classical epic to celebrate 'heroic Tam's' encounter with the supernatural, it effectively democratises literature. The common man is now centre-stage, and his responses are universal; he watches the seductive Cutty Sark in mounting excitement until natural instinct overcomes reason. Crying out in ecstasy he betrays his presence and releases energies that threaten his survival. Paradoxically, by fusing folk-material and the trappings of epic, Burns demonstrates his independent imaginative genius.

In 1795 Burns's health deteriorated: the death of his daughter, Elizabeth Riddell Burns, in September deepened his depression and in the winter he contracted rheumatic fever. A respite in spring 1796 enabled him to resume work on songs.

By early summer, 1796, Burns's condition had worsened and he was nursed by Jean and young Jessie Lewars, for whom he wrote one of his most moving songs, 'O wert thou in the cauld blast'. On the advice of Dr. William Maxwell he spent 3-16 July at Brow, on the Solway, drinking the spa-waters and immersing himself armpit-high in the waters of the firth, probably the worst of all treatments. Maria Riddell

recorded meeting him on 5 July 1796: 'I was struck with his appearance on entering the room. The stamp of death was imprinted on his features. He seemed already touching the brink of eternity. His first salutation was: "Well, madam, have you any commands for the other world?"'.

Burns died on 21 July 1796. On 25 July Jean gave birth to a son whom she named Maxwell (he died before his third birthday). On the same day Burns's cortege passed through the streets of Dumfries to burial in St. Michael's churchyard. Among the citizens lining the streets the question was 'Who will be our poet now?'

Burns's eternity was assured by the wealth of poems and songs that he bequeathed to the world. No writer has been more widely translated. Around the world, gatherings end with the pledge to meet again which is 'Auld Lang Syne'. Of love songs, 'A Red, Red Rose' is surely one of those most often sung. And no poet has surpassed Burns in impacting on the popular consciousness, with some of his lines now part of everyday speech. Ralph Waldo Emerson's words to the Boston Burns Club on the centenary of the poet's birth are fitting epitaph: 'His organic sentiment was absolute independence...He is an exceptional genius. The people who care nothing for literature and poetry care for Burns'.

'AULD LANG SYNE'

Sung around the world, 'auld lang syne' (literally 'old long since/ago') is a celebration of times long past. Burns both claimed to have taken it down 'from an old man's singing' and exclaimed, 'Light be the turf on the breast of the heaven-inspired Poet who composed this glorious Fragment' (i.e. himself). There are precedents in 'Auld Kyndnes foryett' (16th century) and Allan Ramsay's lyric beginning, 'Should auld Acquaintance be forgot./ Tho they return with scars?'. But Burns crafts the universal anthem of friendship that survives separation. A drinking-song, it may also convey nostalgia for an independent Scotland. Stanzas 3 and 4 movingly convey that shared childhood experiences were so meaningful that the speaker virtually relives them in recollecting them; and his awareness of the remorseless movement of time makes him all the more aware of the value of enduring friendship.

Burns Monument & Brig o' Doon by David Roberts, 1862: Burns wrote, 'I had the honor of drawing my first breath almost in the same parish with Mr. Boswell', but he never achieved the meeting with James Boswell that he sought. However it was his son, Sir Alexander Boswell, who presided over the meeting in March 1814 to plan a monument to Burns at his birth-place. Designed by Edinburgh architect, Thomas Hamilton, Burns Monument was opened in 1823. The old Brig o' Doon was in Burns's day the only means of crossing the river. The new road-bridge was built in 1816.

BURNS INFORMATION DIRECTORY

PLACES TO VISIT:

Burns National Heritage Park, Alloway, Ayr

The Burns National Heritage Park, created in 1995, preserves the legacy of Robert Burns and gives an insight into his life and works. The park consists of the cottage where he was born, now with restored interiors, a museum housing personal items, papers and original manuscripts, the Tam o' Shanter Experience Visitor Centre and the Burns Monument. Enthusiasts of the poem Tam o' Shanter can also see Brig o' Doon and Auld Alloway Kirk.

Burns Cottage, Museum and the Tam o' Shanter Experience:
Apr-Sept, 10am-5.30pm.
Oct-Mar, 10am-5pm.
Last entry one hour before closing
Tel: 01292 443700
www.burnsheritagepark.com

Ellisland Farm, near Dumfries

Robert Burns lived and farmed here 1788-1791. It is now a museum containing original writings and possessions. Visitors can join guided tours of the farmhouse and museum or stroll along the banks of the River Nith on Burns Walk, where he was inspired to write many of his works.
Apr-Sept, Mon-Sat, 10am-5pm.
Sun, 2-5pm.
Oct-Mar, Tue-Sat, 10am-5pm.
Closed Sun & Mon.
Tel: 01387 740426
www.ellislandfarm.co.uk

Robert Burns Centre, Mill Road, Dumfries

Situated in an eighteenth century watermill, the centre tells the story of Robert Burns' last years spent in Dumfries. The exhibition features his original manuscripts and belongings and an audio-visual presentation.
Apr-Sept-, Mon-Sat, 10am-8pm;
Sun 2-5pm.
Oct-Mar, Tue-Sat, 10am-5pm.
Closed 1-2pm.
Tel 01387 264808
www.dumfriesmuseum.demon.co.uk

Robert Burns House, Burns Street, Dumfries

The house where Robert Burns spent the last few years of his life and died aged 37 in 1796. Visitors can see the study with his desk and chair, the famous Kilmarnock and Edinburgh editions of his work, original manuscripts and various items belonging to himself and his family.
Apr-Sept, Mon-Sat, 10am-5pm.
Sun 2-5pm.

Oct-Mar, Tue-Sat, 10am-5pm.
Closed 1-2pm.
Tel 01387 255297
www.dumfriesmuseum.demon.co.uk

Globe Inn, Dumfries

High Street, Dumfries
Robert Burns's favourite haunt or 'howff', the Globe Inn has a collection of Burns relics including the chair he used on his visits to the inn. On upstairs windows lines engraved by Burns can still be seen. Several of the rooms have been preserved as they were with fixtures and fittings of the era. Home of the Burns Howff Club, founded in 1889 which celebrates the life and works of Burns. Guided tours of the inn are available during the summer.
Summer: tours at 10.30am, 3pm and 7pm. At other times by arrangement.
Tel 01387 252335
www.globeinndumfries.co.uk

Writers' Museum, Edinburgh

Lady Stair's Close, Lawnmarket, Edinburgh
The Writers' Museum dates from 1622 and showcases personal items, portraits, original manuscripts and Robert Burns's writing desk. The museum also features the writers Sir Walter Scott and Robert Louis Stevenson.
Tel: 0131 529 4901
Fax: 0131 220 5057

Irvine Burns Club & Museum
(see under societies)

Glasgow Vennel Museum Irvine

A museum relating to the period when Robert Burns learnt to dress flax. Also a reconstruction of Burns's 18th-century room.
Fri-Sun, 10am-1pm, 2-5pm.0
Tel: 01294 275059

Souter Johnnie's Cottage, Kirkoswald

John Davidson, who featured in Burns's Tam o' Shanter as Souter Johnnie, once lived in this thatched cottage. Visitors can see furniture of the era, Burns memorabilia, a shoemaker's (souter's) work area and characters from the poem modelled in stone.
Apr-Sept, Fri-Tue, 11.30am-5pm.
Tel: 01655 760603
www.nts.org.uk

Poosie Nansie's Inn, Mauchline

Setting for 'The Jolly Beggars'
21 Loudoun Street
Mauchline Ayrshire KA5 5BA
Tel: (01290 550316)

Burns House Museum, Mauchline

It was in this house, in 1788, that Robert Burns and Jean Armour started married life. The room they lived in now contains an exhibition on Burns.
Easter-Oct, Tue-Sat, 10am-5pm.
Tel: 01290 550045
www.east-ayrshire.gov.uk

Bachelors' Club, Tarbolton

Robert Burns spent time in this seventeenth-century house attending a debating club and socialising.
Apr-Sept, Fri-Tue, 1-5pm
Tel 01292 541940
www.nts.org.uk

SOCIETIES AND INTERNET LINKS:

Burns Howff Club
Tel 01387 261033
www.burnshowffclub.org

Irvine Burns Club & Museum

A Burns club founded in 1826 to commemorate the birth of Robert Burns. The Burns Room tells the story of his life in Irvine with an audio-visual presentation and murals. A Library contains a collection of Burns books, original letters and manuscripts.
Easter-Sept, Mon, Wed, Fri & Sat, 2.30-4.30pm
Oct-Mar, Sat, 2.30-4.30pm
28 Eglinton Street
Irvine KA12 8AS
Tel 01294 274511
www.irvineayrshire.org/burns

The Robert Burns World Federation Ltd
Dean Castle Country Park
Kilmarnock
Ayrshire
KA3 1XB
Tel 01563 572469
Email:
office@robertburnsfederation.co.uk
Web www.worldburnsclub.com

Scotland Online Burns Pages
www.rabbie-burns.com

Robert Burns Country
www.robertburns.org

National Library of Scotland Burns Site
www.nls.uk/burns

The World of Robert Burns
www.robertburns.plus.com

Electric Scotland:
http://www.electricscotland.com/burns/

First published in Great Britain in 2005 by
Colin Baxter Photography Ltd.,
Grantown-on-Spey
PH26 3NA, Scotland
www.colinbaxter.co.uk
Text by Kenneth Simpson
© Colin Baxter Photography Ltd. 2005

No part of this book may be reproduced, stored in a retrieval system or transmitted in any form or by any means without prior written permission of the publishers.
A CIP Catalogue record for this book is available from the British Library.
ISBN 1-84107-284-2
Printed in China